Heartlands

A Collection of Poems

John S. Langley

Copyright © 2024 J. S. Langley

The right of J. S. Langley to be identified as the Author of the Work has been asserted by him in accordance to the Copyrights, Designs and Patents Act 1988. The Copyright for each poem resides with the author. All images are the property of the author or freely available in the public domain

First Published in 2024 by LV Publishing

Apart from any use permitted under UK copyright law, this publication may only be reproduced, stored in a retrieval system, or transmitted, in any form, or by any means, with prior permission in writing of the publisher or, in the case of reprographic production, in accordance with the terms of licenses issued by the Copyright Licensing Agency.

All characters and events in this publication, other than those clearly in the public domain, are fictitious and any resemblance to real persons, living or dead, is purely coincidental.

Print ISBN: 978-1-7391381-8-9

To our sons – Robert, Iain, & Michael, their partners Sophie, Laura, & Kirst, and our grandchildren Abbie, James, Ben & Gabriella who brighten our lives, and to my long-suffering wife, Janet, and my fortunate brothers Robin & Andrew.

John S. Langley

Poetry is the **Heartland** of what creativity and imagination I have left. It gives an outlet to the odd mix of observations, experiences, emotions and thoughts that occur sporadically along the road, in a way that no other artform can. I am very fortunate to be a part of a creative community in the county of Cumbria in the far northwest of England, within a stone's throw of the Lake District National Park to the west, the Pennines to the east and the Scottish Borders to the north, and to draw inspiration from the people, the land, the rich history, and the fears and aspirations of the present and the future. It is with a grateful heart that I offer up this collection – in the hopes that one or two of the pieces may also touch on your own Heartland.

'Heartland: the part considered essential to the viability and survival of the whole.'

CONTENTS

Shards from Life   Page

Sidetracked	2
Nothing Stays the Same	3
Yellow	4
Why?	6
Clapton	8
Gone but not (yet) Forgotten	10
Success	11
Overhead	12
Aqua Vitae	13
70	14
"Good for your age"	15
Spitfire	16
Sweat	18
As it	19
All She Needed	20
TEARS TO CRY	22
Online Departures	23
Margaret	24
Out of Nowhere	26
After	27
Sorry?	28
Moments	30
Journey	32
Will I?	34
First Breath	35
Expectant	36
Birth	37

Can I tell you something…	38
Being Taught By An Expert	39
Cost and Worth	40
Anniversary	43
Passed Over	44
Can we have a 'fast' lane?	46
Perceptions of Value	47
Modern Miracles	48
The Play	50
Common Senses	51
The Last Cast	52
Somewhere Else	54
Cream Tea	56
Reluctant Giver	57
Finding Your Marbles	58
Quo Vadis	59
You	60
Fragile	61
Drone Show	62
Flyover	64
Remember the Best Bits	66

Past Speaks to Present

Churchill Detached	68
All Lumped Together	69
Poppy Dissected	70
Lessons?	71
Ironclad in 2024	72

Here and Then	74
Legacy in Stone	75
Pause a moment	76
Comet	78
The Next 100 Years	80

On Our Way Round

Loch Awe & Kilmartin	82
Inverary Jail	86
Oban	88
Lost and Found	92
It's Sunshine in Scotland	94
Through the Heart of a Valley	96
Exterminate!	100

A Manx Interlude

Getting Started	103
Floating By	104
Modes of Travel	108
Layers and Learning	110
Vikings	114
Yes and No	116
Storyteller	117
Southern 100	118
Laxey Wheel	120
War Wounds	122

John S. Langley

Looking Out, Looking Forward

Monocultures	126
Bystanders	127
Too Much Wet!	128
Please...	129
Aftermath	130
Pointing the Way	134
Bee Contract	136
Peanuts	138
Solar	140
Snowdrops	142
Ringlet	143
I Must Have Said The Wrong Thing	144
Same Place, Different Time	146
What makes You so Special?	147
Night Lights	150
Wings	152
Spotted	154
Moth?	155
Thistle	156
A Troubling Triptych	157
Ordinary?	158
How or Why?	160
Gathering	161
Fieldfare	162
Spider Season	163
Riddle 1,2,3,4	164
Wooden Spoon	166
Seeing is Believing	167

The Pen and The Word

Mastering Words!	170
Show No Fear	171
Don't Wait!	172
Seeking Inspiration	173
Finding The Right Word	174
Legerdemain	175
Life's Work	176
Bon Voyage	178
Halfway Mark	179
Spilt!	180
Afterlife	182
Heartbeat	183
Fiction From Fact	184
Connecting	185
Haiku	187

Shards from Life

John S. Langley

Sidetracked

I stop by a familiar stream
scales scatter in flickering light
as I listen to chattering waters
talking from the past

and I am a child again
searching for otter spraint
lying in the grass unafraid
of bees and muddy knees

until I get home to face
a then that is now past
that I thought would last
forever

I leave the stream to others
walk back to a trodden path
and try to keep my footing
as I walk unsteadily on

Nothing Stays the Same

The place I was conceived has been knocked down
The pub I was born in has changed its name
My first Secondary School is no more
I'm beginning to get a complex

Houses I called home are now occupied by strangers
Family and friends are scattered to the winds
'You can't go back, so much is true
Even though it's part of you.'

Each cell in my body has been systematically replaced
Every seven years or so, a remarkable process
I'm not the same person I used to be
Maybe that's a good thing...

John S. Langley

Yellow

This poem may only be for people of a certain age when Iodine solution was supplied in small bottles with droppers for use as an antiseptic. Drops were either put directly onto the wound or onto a piece of cloth or cotton wool and then applied – each method was equally painful!

When I was young
at least one of my knees
was always yellow

Wearing shorts was the thing
saving the wear and tear on clothing
by exposing the knees

It seemed that everything
worth doing involved
falling and scraping

You got used to the sight
of your own red blood
and the repair process

the wound drying, scabbing, itching
scratching, then a repeat of the error
new scabs for old

Heartlands

The new skin was diaphanous pink
baby smooth and wrinkle-free
needing light and air

But the thing I remember the most
was the sting of the Iodine
the yellowing of the skin

Yeow! It was worse than the wound
A caring mother's method
of combating infection

I came to believe that bright yellow
was the natural colour of
a young boy's knees

Because, when I was young
at least one of my knees
was always yellow.

John S. Langley

Why?

As some kind of resolution
I've often thought
I should have gone back
to my secondary school
with my first class honours degree
and my research prize

I would have showed them
to my teachers and talked about
how times had changed
since they'd predicted my future.
The few who had encouraged me
The majority who hadn't

The times I'd been sent to the
back of the class or the front
or into a corner and told to
keep quiet and behave. It wasn't
their fault I had no aptitude
no ability, and little intelligence

And then I thought - Why?

It would have been good to talk
to those few who had supported me
to thank them to their face for
going above and beyond, for making
a difference, to hopefully give them
something to smile about.
That would have been nice!

Heartlands

But what about the others?
Could I stand those cynical looks
and wry smiles, the little time
they could spare. And when
I reminded them how they used
to put me down, could I stand it

when they told me how happy
they were that such treatment
had turned out to be just the impetus
I'd needed to get my act together.
They'd probably expect me to thank
them for the past humiliations.

I have never gone back.

I sent messages of thanks to a few
    Heartfelt
        In humble deference
            To those who had cared

I swallowed my feelings for the rest.
But sometimes the gall still rises...

John S. Langley

Clapton

There is only one
A guitar slung
Over one shoulder
Eyes closed
Head back

We listen
We move
Cheer
Sweat
Eyes open

What a night!
A legend in Newcastle
Young at heart
Still got it
We both have...

Heartlands

John S. Langley

Gone but not (yet) Forgotten

The ghosts of my past whistle on the wind
As I look over the flattened scree
Of what used to be my school

Here were the solid walls of Victorian brick
The stone steps worn smooth
By scraping schoolchildren

Walls that echoed with the crowd chatter
Each going their own way
Me going mine

I return 40 years later, only 40 years!
To a scene of devastation
A place expunged

No map now shows the good old name
Henry Smith's Grammar
But it yet lives

In dwindling living memory and later
there is the hope of resurrection
(by future archaeologists!)

Success

What's wrong with a personal definition of success?
Finishing a cohesive novel of 90,000 words
Reciting poetry in front of an audience
Being a part of a like-minded group
Learning how to self-publish
Getting one fan letter
Selling a book

Why does my success have to be defined by others?
Selling thousands of books to strangers
Winning several poetry competitions
Attending signings on demand
'Traditionally' published
Reviewed and feted
Exhausted

Why can't anybody believe you're happy with your lot?
No, I mean, that's it, there's no more to say
Why not?...

John S. Langley

Overhead

We live out in the sticks
Between Hardian's Wall
And the Scottish Borders

Surrounded by sheep
Cattle and farms
Life here is never dull

A black bull escaped
At night! Amorously
Pursuing his lady friend

Sheep think anything
In a garden is preferable
To their pastureland

Badgers, deer, hares and moles
And overhead an airshow
Low flying aircraft on
Manoeuvres

Aqua Vitae

From seed and soil it climbs above to fruit
The Sun with water joined in perfect part
to steep and turn, from starch to sugar sweet
then peat smoke dried, hot wetted to the vat

Such special liquor is stirred into a wort
(draff sent elsewhere) and now the yeast
that froths in congeners and alcohol
twice stilled; both by method, and by art

Clear as crystal, raw fire at its heart
through locks to chosen casks transferred
there to sacrifice an angel's part and imbue,
in time, unique colour, flavour and be born

Ah now, behold!
Each dram is worth its weight
So take your time
         and savour every trait...

John S. Langley

70

Slipping silently into seventy
With all my imperfections intact
Virtues polished through to base metal

What matters most is that I made it
No, that's not what matters most
What matters most are the others

Who know me, have put up with me
And still talk to me, despite all
That has happened over the years

Forgiveness is a wonderful thing
But as I get older I realise that
A selective memory
Comes a close second!

"Good for your age"

"You're good for your age"
We're amazed you've not fallen apart
By now

"You're good for your age"
And you've got to be pleased your heart's
Still beating

"You're good for your age"
Cataracts are the least of your worries
Believe me

"You're good for your age"
And as your joints go we can just make you
More and more bionic

If you don't mind waiting awhile
It'll be worth it I'm sure
And soon

It will be hard to know how much of you
Is still there, and how much just needs oiling
Occasionally

During your annual service
If you can get an appointment that is
We're very busy you know

There's a lot like you about…

John S. Langley

Spitfire

A deadly weapon
An invasion thwarted
A culture preserved
For better or worse

A source of pride
An icon in movies
An Airfix kit
A young boy's dream

An Airshow favourite
The Merlin's roar
Superseded now
By the jet engine

A museum piece
Fewer of the few
Still able to fly
These days

A birthday present
To reach for the sky
And alongside see
A Spifire on your wing!

Old men transformed
Into children again
To live out a dream
That was never real

Heartlands

Lost in the mists
Of legend and pride
A country's 'victory'
Symbolised

A day to remember
Reflecting on loss
A past put behind us
But what's all the fuss!?

Our wheels touch the ground
We're back where we started
Is the future we've made
Worthy of the departed?

John S. Langley

Sweat

The honest sweat upon my brow
Not honest but earned, and now

I sit and contemplate my lot
What I've got and what I've not

And realise that the tally's not so bad
I should appreciate the life I've had

And so until my breath returns
I'll sit and be glad in this sunshine
And, in my mind's eye, I'll take the time
to remember, while the flame still burns,

the pleasure of sweat upon my brow
I'm not ready yet to take a bow…

As it

A lady of eighty
Recalling her teens
Reliving the moment
As it was, As it was

A new hip, a swollen leg
Sees herself running
To come second in the race
As it was, As it was

And the boy, Aah the boy
The two of them meeting
Both young and in love
As it was, As it was

So much life in between
Behind those closed eyes
Closed, reminiscing
As it was, As it was

We chat on for hours
Swapping stories and smiles
Then we have to return to
As it is, As it is

John S. Langley

All She Needed

All She needed was an outlet
Most of us do
Someone to vent her feelings to
Often in exaggerated form
And the only one there, on tap
Was her eldest son
It was nobody's fault
Though in later life
She wished that she hadn't

But it was too late by then
To a son who idolised her
Every word she said was true
His father was not a nice man
Though he put bread on their table
And a roof over their heads
For him, his brother and sister
Though he spent little on himself
And smoked his rollies
Down to the last puff

Heartlands

But whatever he did or tried to do
His son could not forgive him
For the stories his mother told

And when, years later
He was the one to discover
His father dead in bed
After a heart attack
My mother asked him
'How did you feel?'
All he could say was
'Regret.'

John S. Langley

TEARS TO CRY

Tears are a blessing
Evolution's way to
Answer the need for a
Release of emotions
Stored up on the inside

Too strong for words
Or ordinary expression

Crying out from your
River of life, an example of
Your (and my) innate humanity

Online Departures

Ken was full of jokes
Inappropriate emails in the main
And I was scared to open
Quite a lot of them!

Sid was a friend and mentor
Half a world away
A man full of wisdom
And a dangerous sense of humour

The internet gave us many years
Of batting banter back and forth
Exchanging smiles across the miles
A little lightness in the chaos

I didn't know how much it meant
Until it stopped
My Inbox was bereft and felt
as dry as autumn leaves

I only have the memories now
Of things I dare not share
Of my friends across the ether
Who I hope knew that I cared

John S. Langley

Margaret

You welcomed us in
Trespassers in your world
Helped us fit it
As much as outsiders
Ever can

Over the years
We got to know you
Had some laughs
Shed some tears
Put the world to rights

You wanted to know
All the goss. You, the fount
Of all useful information
I never left you without
Learning something

You were a master
Of crosswords, an
Armchair champion
Of 'The Chase'
A Great-grandmother

Heartlands

With a shelf full of cards
For every birthday and
When I called in, the kettle
Was always on and, when
Needed, a wee tot of whisky

But only for visitors.
You walked every day
Up to the last few years
Dog obediently (almost)
At your heels

We'll miss you Margaret
Thanks for all your help
We hope you knew how
We felt, though, true to form,
No words were ever spoken.

John S. Langley

Out of Nowhere

It can be a word
Spoken or heard

It can be a smell
Out of nowhere

It can be an image
Planned or unplanned

Or the feel of a place
Of a texture, of skin

Then your body reacts
In reflex, it tenses

Nerves sharpen and
Tingle, eyes water...

There's nothing
You can do

When memory strikes
Like a lightning bolt

Physically
Emotionally

Happy or sad
Good or bad

When memory strikes
You've got to go with it...

                There is no choice.

After

She'd been around all my life
Of course she had
She was my Mother

I knew no world without her
Of course I didn't
She was my Mother

But such logic
does not lead to reason
I go on
though she is gone
She was my Mother

I hear her voice
still loud and clear
'Who is "she",
the cat's mother?'
No, I say,
you were my Mother

John S. Langley

Sorry?

Why do we say sorry
When we burst into tears
As if caring was something
To be embarrassed about?

I was brought up to choke
All the tears away
My father was worse
Of course

Though black and white films
Could bring in a draught
That caught in his eye
That he had to dry

Heartlands

I don't understand
The societal norm
That accepts shouting
And whispering
Laughing and screaming
Talking, in all of its forms
And almost any other
Sort of sound that
The human body can make
But...

Why do we have to say sorry
When we burst into tears
As if caring was something
To be embarrassed about?

John S. Langley

Moments
I.
Sitting in the garden, late April
The Sun is trying to shine
Though the clouds interfere
And it is still cold

Uncertain bees venture out
There is little wind
And I am surrounded by sound
The birds are calling

I stop to listen and enter
A crowded room I usually ignore
All these calls in a language
I cannot understand

My vocabulary and range of
Diction is too inadequate
To record what I hear
I can only listen

There is so much going on!
So many different kinds of call
So much life in progress
And I understand none of it!

My time for sitting is soon over
Too much needs to be done
I must make the most of this weather
And enjoy it while I can...

II.

A Moment
of contentment
takes me
by surprise

The quiet
The tang of salt
upon my tongue

The waves rolling
in breaking lines
of white

The sea, silver
in glittered sunlight
The sky blue
The air still, fresh

A feeling
of calm
sweeps over me

It is only a moment
of welcome
respite

As I turn away
I promise myself
That I will try
to remember
moments like this.

John S. Langley

Journey

The journey South is always long
Hoping for no delays
But this time we were running
To a different clock

Our niece in 'Labour' with her first
My brother anxious
Already 19 hours and exhaustion
Setting in

Texts and calls flew back and forth
And as we finally
Turned into our son's drive
The blessed relief

A healthy son!

Elated we went to share the news
There was an envelope
On the table, addressed to us, inside
The picture of a scan!

Our daughter-in-law was pregnant!
We were speechless
Then full of questions, seeing the joy
On their faces

Heartlands

The next day more driving to get to
Our granddaughter's
First birthday party, lots of balloons
And a card

Read out by her mum, hoping she
Would make a good big sister!
Pregnant! A second daughter-in-law!
We gasped then smiled

Joined in the congratulations
Our heads spinning...

But that's how life is, isn't it?
You wait forever for a bus
And then...

Will I? *(A Mother's question)*

Will I love you, will I care?
A week to go to know
You're there inside me
You, a part of me, for now

The caesarian doesn't bother me
Let them draw the curtain
But when the crying starts
What will my feelings be?

I will do my best, no matter what
I promise you that, right now
But will I love you, will I care?
I dare to hope, but I don't know!

First Breath

I was there at your first breath
The room smelling of disinfectant
And your arrival

I was there as professional hands
Took you and counted toes and fingers
And cleared your nose

I was there to hear the first sound you made
Lamenting the lost warmth of the womb
The cold outside air

I was there when you first met your mother
Snuggled close, hearts feeling the other's beat
Eyes closing, a time to rest

I was there, an impotent bystander
To witness this unique moment of yours
Too absorbed to think of anything else
Except my feelings of relief…

John S. Langley

Expectant *(A Grandparent's prayer)*

Anxiously we wait
These last few days
Hundreds of miles away
But with you as you prepare

What will you look like?
Like all babies I suppose
Alike and uniquely special
Smelling of mother's milk

I cannot, must not, hurry
The hours will look after
Themselves. You will come
In your own good time

I can only lift my hands
To heaven. Please let all
Go well, as anxiously we wait
these last few days…

Birth

Born en caul
In good fortune
A girl

Broken now
A first breath taken
A cry

Unique life
Helpless in newness
Awake

Needing now
Help and warmth
From others

We are here
To give of our best
For you

Welcome Home!

John S. Langley

Can I tell you something…

Can I tell you something?
A four-year-old's hand on my arm
Seeking undivided attention

Sure you can, I say
Clear blue eyes look into mine
Disbelieving

Can I tell you something?
I repeat my answer
And he does

He tells me something

It is a small, but urgent, thing
And I can still feel his
Earnestness

I can still remember the look
On his face

As he taught me something
About giving attention…

Being Taught By An Expert

We share a birthday
A strange coincidence
Only 66 years apart!

We play with each other's presents
(I hide away the Whisky)
We have a go at making jigsaws
Though only one of us is an expert

And it's not me!
'Look out for the edge pieces'
'And the corners'
'We'll do the sky first'

'Can you see the piece I'm missing?'
'Come on Grandad, try harder!'
'I need a T-Rex, and a volcano'
'There it is, pass it over please'

I know my place!
I am guided and controlled
My 66 extra years count for nothing
Against such studious expertise

I could not have imagined such moments
The best of birthday presents
And I hope for more of these jigsaws
That I can be taught to make!

John S. Langley

Cost and Worth

A granddaughter
A sixth birthday

Less easy to pick
A present for
Now

Advice sought
From parents

We're told of
Expensive gifts
Promised by others

But we are directed
To a bracelet making kit

In a pink case.
We do what we're told
For once

On the day, paper is
Ripped, thrown away
Like an upset jigsaw

Heartlands

Clothes are piled in
Unruly stacks, games
Dresses, tiaras, books

Are amongst the many
Treasures at the feet of
Our bossy little princess

Whom we love.

Then she comes to this
One from us...

The wrapping paper goes
The way of all the rest, but
As the contents are revealed

There is
An involuntary squeal

Of delight!

Kids can't fake it!
This is real ... she jumps up
And down in excitement

John S. Langley

And squeals again.

We bask in the reflected
Glow of overexuberance...

Later we reflect
That it's not the cost
That matters

Her reaction, after all
Was priceless

Later still, she makes
The first bracelet for
Her Mother

Plaited in three colours
And on a small plaque

"Love You"

Priceless...

Anniversary

To catch a ray of sunlight in my hand
And hold it there

To hear the sound of running water
And pin it down

To step away from my own shadow
And watch it leave

To stop the wind from blowing

These are things I find impossible to do

Just like describing the feeling I get
when you glance at me
and smile

Nothing more

Just an involuntary gesture

But 46 years on
it means a lot

John S. Langley

Passed Over

The waves are washing over me
And I'm being left behind
I've no computer or internet
I've nothing of that kind

No email and no smartphone
It didn't seem to matter
No Credit Card or Debit Card
So I'm flirting with disaster

I used to be OK with cash
and talking on the phone
to real people at the other end
with that I felt at home

But Siri, Alexa and ChatGPT?
Whatever happened to life?
I can't understand anything
and am increasingly mired in strife

When I talk of my problems
When my feeling are raw
It's like I'm using the language
of a dinosaur

Heartlands

What's happened to talking
walking and cash?
They seem to have gone
all in a flash!

I know I'm old fashioned
and so out of line
But I've got to say this
while there is still time

Remember we're human
and all part of this Earth
let's not lose any more contact
for all that that's worth…

(This poem was AI generated on the theme of 'passed over', spellchecked by Word and rhymed by 'Rhymezone', all available for free on the Internet – or was it?)

John S. Langley

Can we have a 'fast' lane?

Little girls in the Gents toilets
what is the world coming to?
Is there no privacy anymore?
Not even in the loo

I'm all in favour of the modern man
And supporting minorities too
But what about us older men
Who repeatedly need the loo?

Can we install a fast lane?
As fast as the old can go!
Somewhere to park a Zimmer
in order to soften the blow

I've nothing against fathers
with daughters they want to help
I just want to avoid any problems
that end with me shouting 'yelp!'

The time will come when you youngsters
are no longer young yourselves
So please consider us 'oldies'
As you'd like to consider yourself!

Perceptions of Value

Whatever we can do
We tend to undervalue
And what we're really bad at
And others get off pat
We are amazed and greet with awe
Believing that what we just saw
Is somehow superhuman
Well above our own abilities

But others may also look on us
Wondering in all the fuss
How we do what we can do
That they believe of value
And we, disbelieving it at best
See it as an awkward jest
And look only on our weaknesses
Just as most other people do...

John S. Langley

Modern Miracles

We are the privileged
with replacement joints
so we can walk again
Cataract operations
so we can see again
Cochlea implants
to help us hear

And for me
a heart operation
up through a keyhole
in a shaven groin
a small camera
a television screen
a ringside seat
and lasers!

A catheter ablation to
combat tachycardia
words from
a Medical Dictionary
that mean little to me
other than something
is wrong and
I need help!

Heartlands

And help there was
the Consultant asked,
"Why do you want this
operation?". I replied
that I would like a chance
to meet my grandchildren
if there were any!

And now I have, four of
them, bright as buttons
and twice as cheeky!
I am lucky that strangers,
with their skills, have
granted me this time
given me this opportunity!

Though they may never
read this, I just wanted
to say
          THANK YOU...

John S. Langley

The Play

The play is the same
The lines centuries penned
Carved in literary stone

I learned them decades ago
Passed exams dissecting them
Exclaimed them in several productions

But now, for some reason
They play with me
Dance around my memory
Jig playfully on the page

And I have to be prompted
Reminded of what I've always known
What is happening?

Why has the world changed?

Heartlands

Common Senses

Wow!
Isn't it amazing
I can taste this air I breathe
I can see a rainbow of colours around me
I can feel my heart beneath my skin, beating in my chest
I can smell the perfumes of this wild world
I can hear, stand still and listen
Isn't it amazing
Wow!

I hope future generations have
this same simple opportunity
and I strive to hold onto enough faith
to believe that this can be so
And if in this world there is faith, hope and love...

    ... let us harness the greatest of these...

John S. Langley

The Last Cast

My brother's fly, black and silver
Fished just below the surface
After a day of disappointment
And the light fading

Casting under an overhang
As instructed by a friend
Who knew the waters
It was worth a try

Anything was!
And then a pull on the line
A take and a strike
A tight line!

I brought the fish in
Avoiding the reeds
Giving and taking line
Close to the edge

Heartlands

My brother manned
The Landing Net
The fish dodged
Then was captured

The fly removed
A photo taken
The fish returned
Safely to the water

A collaborative effort
The fish, me, my brother
Our friend of many years
At the end of a long day

Success came at last
Fleeting but magical
A moment to remember
Like life…

John S. Langley

Somewhere Else

I should have been somewhere else
But I wasn't
A mixture of apathy and illness
was to blame
In my mind at least

So I fixed the gear stick on my car
with PTFE tape
got the convertible roof working again
but I don't know how.
I checked in on the bees

who were pollen-laden, a good sign
I thought
I read some of Paul Muldoon's poetry
cryptically kind words
and understood some

of the digressions. Did you know that
a hippo
can run at 19 mph if it wanted to?
Which normally
it doesn't...

Heartlands

Using steps I cleared the garage gutter
clogged with moss
and unintentionally located a wasp's nest
which I left alone
(perhaps for another time?)

I watered the chillies, that thrive on neglect,
and sprinkled
the painfully slow-growing ginger lightly
in hope but not
expectation

I took a walk, the mixed scents of wild
flowers wafting
over me in a language I couldn't begin
to understand
so I sat down

I should have been somewhere else
but sometimes
being somewhere you're not supposed
to be
is not so bad…

John S. Langley

Cream Tea

Even a cream tea
is something over which
we always disagree

Such a simple pleasure
but rooted in local culture
it's anything but leisure

It's sc-on not sc-own!
It's sc-own not sc-on!
It's jam then cream!
It's cream then jam!

If Gulliver were watching on
he'd understand the barney
though it hasn't yet led to war
there is no room to parley

If we can get so entrenched
over such a simple thing
what chance have we to coexist
in peace and harmony

Let us, my friends, decide for once
that any way you do it
a real cream tea is a thing of joy
and, with gratitude, go to it!

Reluctant Giver

Why is it so difficult to part with something
And so much easier to acquire and hold?

Does everyone feel the same way about it
Or is it just me who is bad at doing this?

Things I don't really need anymore, but
Then again might come in handy sometime

You never know do you? Just after it's gone
Is probably the time you'll need it most

Just like the thing... but stop... come on!
You've got to learn how to part with stuff

It may not be easy, you might not want to
But things can weigh you down you know

OK, now's the time. No time like the present
Here please take this poem...
　　　　　　　　...before I change my mind.

John S. Langley

Finding Your Marbles

Black cat, sharp claws
sharp teeth, swipes out
We pass on that one

A cat from the back
walks out of the shadows
down an inclined ramp

Rubs against our legs
Is stroked
Purrs

'She doesn't normally do that
Keeps herself to herself
Sits on her own, she's very shy
Of people

Called Phoebe
Owned by an old lady
Who has died
They think she's been grieving
But that's crazy isn't it
Cats don't grieve

We had not chosen a cat
A cat had chosen us
She was a tortoiseshell
We renamed her Marbles
She didn't seem to mind.

Quo Vadis

'Wither goest thou?'
Asked the young woman with the cow
In her hands

'I go to market,' I replied
Hoping she'd not know I lied
With a straight face

'And what do you there?'
She asked, speaking through her hair
Long and dark, and pure

'I go to sell this special hen,'
Showing it to her there and then
From under my overcoat

'I'll buy it with a kiss,' she said
And her words went straight into my heart
And I acquiesced

Now I must go home again
But without my special hen

The girl is gone I know not where
The girl who had the long, dark hair

I'm sure my mother will understand
It's my father I'm worried about!

John S. Langley

You

I wasn't expecting it
I was doing OK
Just on a night out
With my mates

Expecting nothing
But a few laughs
A bit of fun
At the weekend

Then I saw you…
And everything changed.

Fragile

And I said:
"Take my heart
But be careful
It's fragile
Please don't
Break it."

And she said:
"Take mine too
It's for you
If you want it
Please don't
Break it."

And our two hearts
Beat in time
Looking at
Each other
And sighed
As one

Still fragile
Intertwined
We take 1 day
At a time
Eyes closed
Fingers crossed…

John S. Langley

Drone Show

Dinosaurs fill the night sky
Outlined by obedient drones
Glowing red, white, and green

The queuing for food takes
longer than the show lasts!
But is worth it, in the end

Is this the end for fireworks?
More environmentally friendly
Less bangs, jeopardy and smoke!!

The speed and maneuverability
is more frightening, you could
not escape if chased by a drone

Used for less friendly purposes
this latest technology opens the
way for new forms of devastation

Used well, there is opportunity
delivering blood in record times
making education fun, surveying

from the air, movie making...
As always it's up to us - I just
look up into the night sky
and watch a dinosaur...

Heartlands

John S. Langley

Flyover

It's the noise you hear first
The rising roar of approach

The surprise and anticipation
Sharpens the senses

Eyes follow the sound
Searching the sky

And then it's there!
Flying low

Four engines
Military transport

A training flight
Passing over

I watch it leave
Sound receding

Size diminishing
Air closing in behind

It's the sight you lose last
The memory you retain

But did it happen at all?
Is this story true?

Heartlands

John S. Langley

Remember the Best Bits

I know I can be cantankerous
grouchy and irritating too
But what I'd like you to do
is remember some of the best bits.

It's easy to remember the frailty
of the last days and the last time
But it really isn't a crime
to also remember the best bits

There were some you know
plenty to raise a laugh or a smile
Nice to pause and think for a while
of some of the best bits

The best bits are what I'd prefer
that people choose to recall
if I'm remembered at all
...and that would be one of the best bits

Aye, that would be one of the best bits

Past Speaks to Present

John S. Langley

Churchill Detached

Churchill radio speeches on vinyl
Hard black, round and grooved
The words hidden in the trenches

And now we listen at our leisure
If we listen at all. It is a history
With the constant threat removed
And we no longer comprehend

Though the words are the same
The lisp heard through the static
The promise of hope dripping out
Onto the lounge carpet

But then it mattered, you see
Each word there to be hung upon
Like a lifeline of straw to a future
That seemed very far away

Is it so with all our words?
Each in their laboured moment
Lost or remembered out of place
Is this why we learn so little
From the past?

All Lumped Together

The so-called 'Iron Age' lasted
700 years or there abouts
and we look on it as if there
were consistency throughout
as if there were a clear beginning
and the transparency of an end.

The Romans were in some parts
of what they called 'Britannia'
for more or less 400 years
and we consider all of it as a
consistent continual occupation
from arrival to departure.

It's like saying that we are now
just the same as those first
Elizabethans; that we dress
the same, eat the same,
live as long, that there has
been no Industrial Revolution.

Seems to me that it's all more
complicated, that the complexity
is more than we can cope with
so we oversimplify, and pretend to
understand. Now I can only wonder how
we might be described in 500 years' time?

John S. Langley

Poppy Dissected

The poppy is a weed
growing on disturbed ground
with petals that have evolved
to attract pollinators

They are not meant
to signify the colour of blood
and would answer to any name
in silence, just the same

It is we who have imposed
a meaning where there is none
It is not an uncommon deed
to satisfy a human need

If it were not the poppy, with
its own black heart, we would
choose something just as simple
to elevate to a National symbol

that we copy in paper or plastic
and wear but once a year
in remembrance of folly oft repeated
a remembrance that I hope is more real

Lessons?

Bare now and fallen
stone that was hewn and shaped
is now scattered, re-used, littered
or is re-absorbed into the soil

Forged high the Wall, a symbolic
man-made line, a physical symbol of
a foreigner's power over topography

A control exerted, in all directions
North and South on straight roads
East and West along the line

that crossed rivers, forests, and fields

Built, it was, to last for a forever
of over three hundred years
So many lifetimes and generations
that it became immutable to all

who lived in its shadow.

Now, almost 2,000 years later
we look upon these mighty works
not in despair...
        ...but in its state of ruin

John S. Langley

Ironclad in 2024
A musing on the monument to Roman Occupation at Wallsend (Segedunum)

Ironclad in history
In a language
They did not speak
Anchored

Four hundred years
Pushed between pages
All logical and
Homogeneous

Like saying that
The world of 1624
Was the same
As ours today

What monument
Will stand for us
And will it last as long
As this Cold Iron?

Heartlands

John S. Langley

Here and Then

One short million years ago
Rhinos, Hippos and herds of Bison
Roamed the land we now call Britain
Rivers flowed in unfamiliar beds
Before Man stepped out unshod

Bodies fell in mud and mire and hid
Anaerobically, hardening the arteries
To stone. Sunk in the sands of time
Until rising to stand before the sea
The eroding tides of rediscovery

Laid bare for new age beachcombers
To piece together, in disbelief, a past
Preserved from warmer climes and in
The lab to analyse a frozen human
Footprint that would fit a shoe size 9

Legacy in Stone

Red sandstone
200 million years
in the making
quarried and cut
by younger hands
over our years
of changing ideas

The same stone
obediently re-shaped
to fit the fashion
is here re-laid
old style under new
a new layering.
An historical legacy

Then itself rediscovered
by later eyes
and coldly debated
The warmth of those
that laid/re-laid them
having passed
long since

And what of future eyes?
If the stones outlast
the weathering
what, if anything,
will they believe
our time was like
our style...
      ... our stonemasonry

John S. Langley

Pause a moment

It must have been warm in here
Here where the ovens were
Here the four storeys
The large fireplaces

Here where the wind now whoops
And the swallows swoop
Between the vanished floors
Riding the present draughts

There must have been footsteps here
Treading the boards overhead
And lavish meals served up
Amidst lively conversation

Heartlands

Here where the walls now echo
To the sound of tourist's feet
Necks craning to see the sky
Through the missing roof

There must have been fighting here
Harsh words, the clash of steel
Here where history was forged
Century upon century

Here where the silence can be heard
Between the fleeting visits of
People who are passing through
Before hurrying on to the next thing…

John S. Langley

Comet

See me low
in the afterglow
of the setting Sun

I have returned
after 80,000 rounds
of what you call years

The Neanderthals
would have seen me then
if they'd looked

And now your eyes
(still 2% Neanderthal)
may see me tonight

But look up soon
before I disappear
back into the dark

I wonder
when I next return
in 80,000 years

Will there be eyes to see
and will those eyes
be 2% human?

Heartlands

John S. Langley

The Next 100 Years

In one lifetime
The first manned flight
To landing on the Moon

Two World Wars
One General Strike
And Colour TV

So what will you see
Born in 2024?

I hope it is generally good
But who knows?

Who could have foreseen
What came before

So what chance do we have
Of predicting the future?

Heartlands

On Our Way Round

John S. Langley

Loch Awe & Kilmartin
(March 2024)

Wearing winter quilted wraps
against scalding Scottish winds
ice sharp against our exposed skin
piercing through our pinkness
we walk a path badly signed
and go wrong

Lost and forlorn we flounder
through field, and stream and bog
dodging beasts protecting calves
shooing sheep, finding white skulls
turning back, uncertain where
we went wrong

Although we did not find the
ancient rock art cupped and ringed
that had lain static for millennia
but forever hidden from us
our thousands of steps were not
all in vain

Heartlands

We returned to the car park
needing coffee and warmth
but can find no shops open.
It makes us consider what life
is like here, here in this part
of our country

It must be a communal existence
with mutual help a necessity
a trading of favour for favour
keeping tally in a mental purse
of debits and credits:
> *A school run for a school run*
> *A loaned chainsaw for a meal*

We consider how much we take
that is so easily lost

Later, we find ancient cists,
cairns, and still standing stones
aligned, circled, placed, fallen
once giving meaning, protection
indecipherable to us today

John S. Langley

A body leaves only a pale
phosphate shadow behind
but stones are moved, removed,
replaced, reused or resurrected
colonised slowly by creeping
moss and lichen

Amidst all this the sheep graze
geese gather, ready to leave.
Green streamers, like a lithe mane,
wave beneath crystal clear water
that flows on, from then to now
and onwards towards a tomorrow
when we have gone...

We leave
We leave nothing
We leave nothing but memories
We leave nothing but memories and a little DNA
Behind us

Heartlands

John S. Langley

Inveraray Jail

It is a dreich day. We visit a jail
To learn how brutal punishment was
Stocks, hangings, floggings, burnings.
We try a thumbscrew
It hurts!

Now dry and neat, in their time
The cells were dark, damp, and dour
Cramped and crowded
Good for growing
Disease

That was 150 years or so ago.
Today a guide is dressed in prison garb
Another as a Warden. We talk about
Discipline in schools today
Compared to ours

There are designated areas for exercise
One hour a day, a welcome break from work
10 hours a day shredding old rope to oakum
Hard on the fingers, doing 5 lbs a day
To stuff mattresses

Or caulk the gaps in marine planking.
Along the corridor another prisoner weaves
Herring nets. More skilled, easier on the hands.
In time men's and women's blocks are separate
A model for other prisons.

Heartlands

Some escape, but few remain free for long.
There is no leniency in the law for children
Or pregnant women. Prisoners are washed, fed
Taught. There is a doctor. For some it is better
Than living outside

It is an extremely good tour with audio guide
Eye opening and thought provoking. Nothing
Is black and white. There is harshness amidst
A world that is changing. We escape into the
dreich outside and welcome the cool of the rain
        ...the freedom to leave when we like...

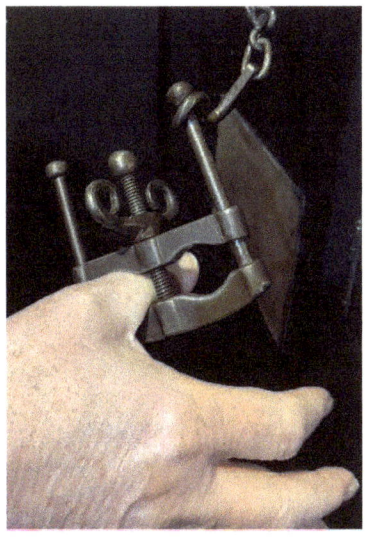

John S. Langley

Oban

Lots of things change in 47 years
The loose grit of the car park is gone now
smoothed to tarmac, but the boat tours
are still clustered here, bobbing by the dock
touting their excursions

But today no one is stupid enough to
jump aboard, at the very last minute,
an eight hour round trip on turbulent waters
to Eigg, Rum, Muck, and Canna with no overcoat
in biting salt winds, no food and nothing hot to drink

I can still hear the justified complaints of
my Irish travelling companion who kept asking
'What are we doing?' and 'Why are we doing it?'
'Please enlighten me!' One thing was for sure
There was no turning back

Once started, you couldn't just change your mind
and get off! We had to grin and bear it, watch others
warmly wrapped, open their pre-prepared lunch boxes
stuffed full, pour steaming drinks from thermos flasks
and cast us pitying looks, but no crumbs!

Heartlands

Landfall brought a small store, but no hot drinks
no sandwiches! We bought Mars bars, crisps
and fizzy drinks. We emptied our pockets to
buy a woolen blanket to share, and recharged
ourselves with liquid, salt and sugar.

A little refreshed and off again, more chocolate
secreted about our person. Once bitten twice shy.
The wind eases, splinters of light scatter and silver
the waves, breaks in the cloud reveal blue in a
brightening sky

We hunt for shafts of sunshine, raise our faces
to bask in its warming ultraviolet rays
and the trip now becomes an adventure
We talk to people, we laugh, we walk on
unknown islands

We see the rich birdlife, appreciate their resilience
which is far beyond our own, and on the way back,
as the boat heaves from trough to crest, we share
the thick blanket, brave the elements
with better sea legs.

John S. Langley

Our craziness has given others a tale to tell
Let them! They are onlookers. This is our story.
We lived it, like the birds we watch dive into cold
waters, we recognize we are outsiders here, dipping
pink toes into a different world

We watch as they seek sleek fish... not Mars bars!
Back and tethered in Oban we leap ashore
run for the car and pull on our warm coats,
left thoughtlessly in the boot, and shiver our way
to increased body heat

And then we buy tea, cupping our hands for
maximum ceramic warmth, our teeth chattering
'That was so stupid!' says my friend, smiling.
'But you've got to admit,' I reply, 'It was worth
Doing. Now that we know we've survived.'

I get a shrug in reply. All things considered
it is the kindest reaction I could have hoped for.
Now, 47 years later, I'm on a different adventure.
Everything is different
                        but nothing has changed.

Heartlands

John S. Langley

Lost and Found

Driving North from Oban
To get a glimpse of Appin
A stronghold of the Stewarts
Though centuries ago

Located on an islet
Accessed by a boat
Lies bonny Castle Stalker
just trying to keep afloat

We're following a map now
Not sure which way to go
We've jettisoned the Satnav
And rely on what we know

And so we travel onwards
Passing through Glencoe
The valley deep and windy
The tops still glazed with snow

So much history in the offing
Stories rich but insincere
We drive onwards to the future
Wondering what has brought us here

Heartlands

John S. Langley

It's Sunshine in Scotland

It's sunshine in Scotland
We emerge into Edinburgh
Tumble from the tram
By the Scott Monument
No raincoat on our back

It's a big risk!
But the sky is blue
The forecast optimistic
And it is Festival month
Teeming sidewalks, dodging

Rucksacks, elbows, cracked
Paving, surviving the crush
To follow your interests
Opera, Books, Film, Fringe
The choice overwhelming

Heartlands

Ticket prices rising!
Looking out for 2 for 1's
Starting to sweat in 25 degrees
Wet even on a dry day!
Drowning in Creativity

It's sunshine in Scotland
From morning till dusk
The temperature cools
And it's time to go home
But it's still not raining!

John S. Langley

Through the Heart of a Valley

We travel regularly through the Lune Gap, the Howgill Fells to the East, and each time it is different, driven by the colours of the seasons and the weather (Sun, rain and cloud), but always it is awe inspiring. Recently a small timber plantation has been planted in the shape of a heart, sitting gently on the rising slopes of the Howgill Fells - it always makes us smile...

We Pass through the Lune Gap
Manchester bound on the M6
Musing on origins

Molten at first
Moulded by heat
And tectonic forces

Cooling to crystallise
Folding and buckling
Hard as rock

Then worn down, crumbled
By wind and rain
Creating soil

Heartlands

Birthing new colour
As roots find a purchase
And green spreads

Until the Ice comes
looking for a weakness
grindingly slow

Carving a way through
The first cut deepened
Scouring width

Leaving a river to snake
A meandering vein
Of life support

Later animal tracks
Criss-cross under trees
Four feet then two

Homes, hamlets, farms
Pause then stick
Become rooted

John S. Langley

Walls and fences demarcate
Though streams break through
The heathered grazing

Wheels rut, trains track
Wires traverse overhead
Tarmac smooths

Hard rock is re-exposed
Where man-made routes
Are exploded through

Artificial order imposed by mapping
An artwork of contour lines
Unevenly spaced

And recently a tree plantation
In the Shape of a Heart
Staked and tubed

Over the years we watch it grow
Trapping the weather
Holding the cloud

Memory and time held in place
Solid and ethereal joined
The Heart of a Valley

Heartlands

John S. Langley

Exterminate!

A gathering of graphic novel artists
On the shores of Windermere
Under canvas

At the end of September in sunshine
An International confabulation
Where the talented gather

We design our sandwich for lunch
From a choice of breads and
Multifarious fillings

We consume our creations in the midst
Of the banquet of aptitudes that
Abound around us

Marvel, DC, Classics, fresh approaches
We are overwhelmed and then
We see a Dalek!

Gliding past tourists queuing for cruises
The genuine article from the TV
Created reality

I have to look twice, to believe my eyes
Then decide to make an approach
Very cautiously

Heartlands

Here is where fantasy and reality meet
As, in broad Yorkshire, the Dalek said
'Hello luv ... Exterminate!'

John S. Langley

A MANX INTERLUDE

Heartlands

Getting Started

A new Port for us
a fixed time of departure
We play it safe and arrive far
too early, better that than late
though everything is closed!

We navigate to
a coffee machine
Cash free and complicated
nurse the black liquid
of unknown origin

The queue is packed
with eager motorcyclists
All ages and polished chrome
who talk of past visits
and things to be avoided

The loading and unloading
is a pit stop masterclass
of maneuvering heavy loads
into ever tighter corners
still leaving room for us

We board MV Manxman
less than a year old
new luxury; cafe, bar, restaurant
good coffee and sausage rolls
And the sea is calm!

John S. Langley

Floating By

Time to enjoy the journey over
Cormorants like sentries see us out
Gannets forage for fish in full flight
black-tipped wings folding smoothly back
as arrow-sharp they spear the sea

Blackpool Tower and the Big Dipper
edge the far shore, standing sentinel
to pleasure and entertainment while
a yacht's white sails skirt the wind and
chubby chugging cargo-carriers churn
froth and foam from old diesel engines
sheepishly avoiding the sleek speedsters
whose white hulls hurry home

We search between the sprinkled stars
of light that sparkle the water's surface
looking for the sharp-wet fins of dolphins
slicing the skin of this calm crossing but
see nothing and turn inwards...

This metal should not float. We are held here
by the power of the ignored, essential, unseen
The transparent lightest of things that creates
buoyancy. Air. Keeping the heaviest ship afloat

Heartlands

'It's not always like this,' we're told
'Some crossings can be rough indeed.'
We believe it, and appreciate our luck

Outside the open sea is open no more
Man-made change is strung across half
the horizon in the form of wind turbines
harvesting the wind to work an elemental
transformation. A telltale tri-blade turns
like a clock face, taking its slow rotational
time to change the invisible into electricity

An oil platform sits steadily on its stilts
A new island, creating new iron habitats
below the surface, pumping the past to
the surface for today's dubious uses that
alter fragile balances, in the wrong direction.

Our time passes, we go forward, not back.
Even if we turned around, we would return
to a different world. Nothing stays the same.

Out of the sea, below a tablecloth of cloud
a strip of undulating land appears, still far
shimmering in tantalisingly opaque solidity

John S. Langley

We crawl closer, cliffs climb between blue
and blue. We appear to drift, surrounded by
the noise of a mixed school trip, step over
multi-coloured metallic motorcycle helmets
looking like the severed heads of lost souls,
mouths open, taking in no breath of air.

Slumbering bodies begin to shift, there is
increasing activity as we travelers awaken
from the suspended animation of journeying.

The Port appears. The ship pirouettes to dock
and we prepare to disembark, and return to
our vehicles. Ropes are thrown and tied off
ramps are lowered. Our wheels turn...

The time has slipped by. We have aged 3hrs
and 45mins, which is long enough to know that
we have traded a departure for a destination
We have had time to consider, to be interested,
to be tired, to be bored, always with an end in
view. Unknown. Unvisited. Previously beyond
our touch. Is it better to continue travelling in
hope than to arrive?
Only time will tell...

Heartlands

John S. Langley

Modes of Travel

I.
À pied
Each step
a new adventure

II.
A large Shire Horse
draws a carriage
along the promenade
in Douglas
the muscular build
of its haunches
one horse power

III.
The Electric Railway
Overhead wires
Old carriages
Hard seats
To Ramsey
on a rainy day

IV.
A Mountain Railway
crawls skyward
summits Snaefell
the highest point
at over 620m
atop a kestrel's hover
looking out to seek
a view of 5 kingdoms

Heartlands

V.
A Single-decker bus
to Port Erin
diverted round the
Southern 100 course
over scenic lands
How many horses
does it take
to power
a Diesel engine?

VI.
The Steam Train emits
remembered smells
and sounds
Polished chrome
from Erin to Douglas
such power and whistles

VII.
The Transport Ferry
in new Manxman luxury
towards home
Over our shoulder
a Sunset

John S. Langley

Layers and Learning

I.
Small family groups
each living off the land
taking what they need
afraid of bears and wolves

Sustainable garnering

Life may be shorter
but there is still time
to love, to look, to be
conscious of good fortune

Now that time is gone, over.
Like Electronic Calculators
are now obsolete

II.
Farming the land
putting down roots
stone and wood tools
storage and seeds

Sustainable rotation
Increased impact

Building, weaving
breaking, cutting
defence, attack

Proceeded like the
Video Cassette

Heartlands

III.
Fire and ore
Metalworking
Moulding
Technological breakthrough!

Limited by resources
Precious materials

Improved tools
Greater productivity
Larger communities

Old fashioned like
Desktop Computers

IV.
Religion and writing
Spreading of knowledge
Recording of history
Cities and Towns
Moving away from the land
Connections weakened
No limits perceived

Just as the light of a star
reaches us after it has died
so writing from the past
reaches us from a world
already gone and unknowable

And so we move on
Into a world of mobile phones
where the future is AI…

First Metalworkers
Celtic Farmers
First Farmers
Hunter Gatherers
First Christians
The Manx Evidence
A.D.
B.C.

1a
1b
1c
1d
2
3a
3b
3c
4
5
6a
6g
6h

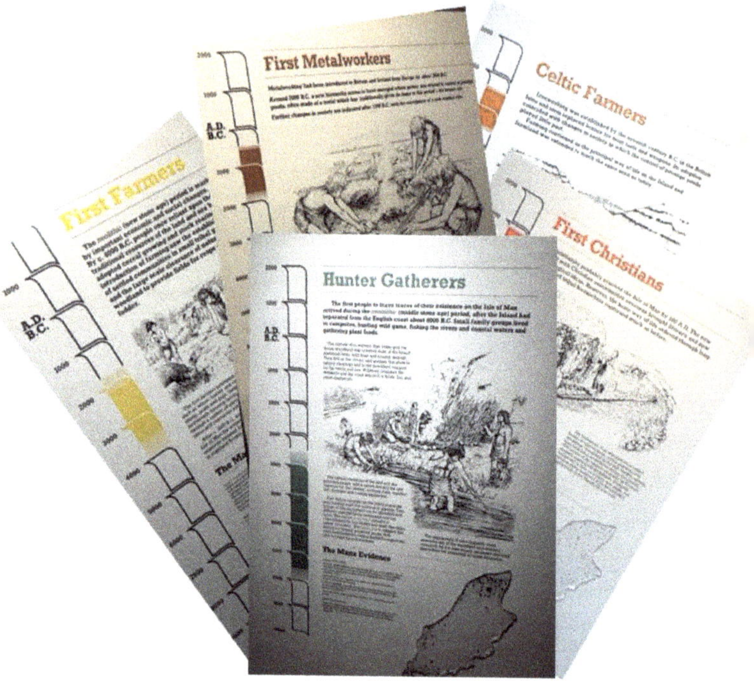

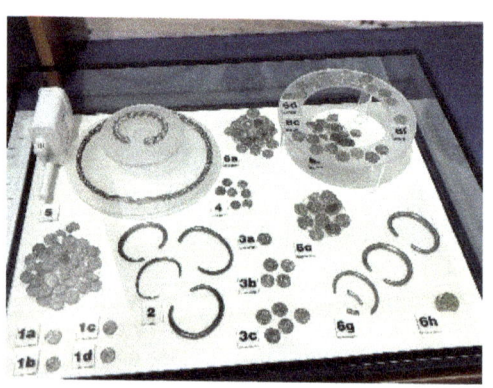

Heartlands

V.
We are like no other creature
on this sphere of life
generation to generation
growing in capability
until it is too much

Reaching limits
at first in ignorance
then knowingly
needing to listen
act consciously
collaboratively
LIKE NEVER BEFORE...

We'll have no choice!

John S. Langley

Vikings

There were no Romans here!
But trade brought us pirates
ravens on a salt-scented wind
and a more favourable tide
trading in their own beliefs
speaking differently to the Celts
carrying sharp swords

And with this rose the value
of a shiny metal
too soft to hold an edge
that becomes a currency instead
- why not?

And so they (as us) come to covert
something they can't eat
but can count, stamp
exchange, the first Manx coinage
or work into ornament, bowls, cups...

There is assimilation
but not amongst equals
and a new amalgam emerges
that still sits right at the heart of things
today.

Treasure and Trade

Trade first brought the Vikings to the Isle of Man. The Viking Age is the **first** time that we see large amounts of **currency** on the Island and the first Manx **coinage**. This evidence of their financial transactions points to the Island being a centre of **wealth** and **commerce**.

John S. Langley

Yes and No

You won't find Badgers
Grey Squirrels or Moles
Oh no!
They're not here
not there, not anywhere
not here!

But you will find animals
unique and special
and these are here
oh yes they are!

The Manx cat
all black and white
without a tail
but that's alright

The Loaghtan sheep
wool brown and deep
four horns on its head
to show its well bred

Red-necked wallabies
yes, really it's true
escapees who've settled
smaller than a kangaroo

So when you visit
The Isle of Man
remember we're special
and enjoy it while you can

Storyteller

An old man in flickering light
outside a storm is raging
sits and speaks

"You are part of my dream
I am a dream within your dream"

He tells of Sigurd and the Dragon
how he learns the language of birds

*Outside the storm subsides
and over the silent sea
Manannan's cloak drifts in.*

John S. Langley

Southern 100

We leave the train at Castletown
to the roar of racing motorbikes
and follow the rising noise
to a coned-off crossroad
and join the crowd

We listen to the announcements
watch as the bikes flash past.
Two back out of the corner
on separate laps
and then...

A riderless bike scrapes menacingly
along the tarmac, on its side
out of control, at speed
slicing air, too fast
to dodge...

A Marshal is in the way, is cut down
thrown forward headfirst, cracks
her head against the road
All in slow motion, then
speed of action...

Red flags, paramedics, ambulances
blue lights, all racing paused
everyone clear on their role
as if this were a familiar
routine...

Heartlands

For us there is nothing familiar about it
but also, there is nothing we can do
except get out of their way
which we do
promptly...

Later we hear there were no serious injuries
although two days earlier there were
and the year before two fatalities.
We scratch our puzzled heads
and leave them to it...

John S. Langley

Laxey Wheel

Mining beneath the surface
Below the water level
Silver, Lead and Zinc ore
There for the taking
If you can get the men

Less problem than
the greedy depth
That needs pumping
2,000 feet down
250 gallons a minute

A 72 foot wheel
6 feet wide
water driven
raising water
Turning 3 times a minute

And today we climb
the spiral staircase
to the top platform
holding tight
feeling exposed

This is no place
for the faint hearted
Engineering marvel
Hard iron protector
of soft flesh, strong wills

Heartlands

John S. Langley

War Wounds

On the Ferry home we overhear
Bikers telling their stories
Comparing injuries
Past crashes

Long journeys in bad weather
Sleeping under leaky canvas
Getting to trial meets
In obscure places

These men are no Spring Chickens!
Who now compare old wounds
Weeks in traction
Near misses

It is like eavesdropping on an Anatomy
Class; crushed bones, torn sinew
Metal plates, screws and scars
Living to tell the tale

Memories of lost friends. The adrenaline
rush that keeps them coming back
for more, even though they
know they shouldn't

Their wives and partners are supportive
understand it's not just sport
but something deep seated
in their psyche

Heartlands

They grimace when they rise for the toilet
or to go to the bar for another beer (or two).
They talk about what happened this year
and look forward to the next

If there is one...

John S. Langley

Looking Out, Looking Forward

John S. Langley

Monocultures

Monocultures just don't work
Becoming top dog might feel good
But never lasts

Diversity is where it's at
Taking out and putting back
Each to its own

Artificial support shores it up
Chemicals and ingenuity
A false sense of security

We've come this far, why change tack?
Is an arrogant strategy
With finite limits

Being less in control
Might be tough on the ego
But that's how it is

We'd be better learning
How to cohabit
You never know

We might even enjoy it!

Bystanders

We are observers
Of other people's trials
From a distance

Intellectually dissecting
Other people's distress
Looking on

It only really matters
When it is our trauma
Our pain

When that world is
All of a sudden, ours
With no escape

Then we don't understand
Why everyone else doesn't
Feel our pain as we do

Why there is no outpouring
Of sensible, practical action
To stop each other hurting

But that is not the way.

We look on
From a distance
Expert bystanders…

John S. Langley

Too Much Wet!

Please, give me three dry days in a row
The fields are sodden and overflowing
The rivers are high and grinding out
new paths

The moles are not burrowing but
doing a breaststroke
Please give me three dry days in a row

I don't mind the cold, I'll even take wind
as long as the gusts are under
40 mph

Just let it be dry
Please let it be dry, O
Please give us
three dry days in a row!

Heartlands

Please...

This land was tended, within its means
For centuries

Crop rotation, nutrients returned from
The animals it fed

Mankind's understanding honed to
A fine cyclical art

Thinking long term, passing on from
One generation to the next

Until Productivity, Efficiency and Now
Became the order of the day

Do not push me too far, there is
An edge over which

I can fall, a point of no return
Do not push me that far

Please...

John S. Langley

Aftermath

24 hours on
the storm has past
the high tide powered
by strong winds
has receded.

So many starfish
have been stranded
crabs, whelks, muscles
are dashed upon
the rocks.

Rocks scoured clean
of everything
and everything piled
in mounds of
marine debris

Heartlands

Cockles crust
a new tideline
crackling and spitting
on the shore, still living
but adrift of anchorage

They must hold on
if they can
wait
for the next tide
to take them back

Meanwhile Gulls feed
and a twisted groyne
is in an agony
of anguished defiance
to escaping sand

John S. Langley

that now dunes
on the promenade.
This is the time
for some kind
of recovery

slower
than the speed
of destruction
wrought
and then gone

until the next time...

Heartlands

John S. Langley

Pointing the Way

It was a sign, the people said
That heaven would fall upon their head
That darkling bird with beady eye
Was pointing upwards, to the sky

They shoo-ed it and they shot at it
That bird of such ill omen
But on that signpost it would sit
Each and every morning

They blamed it for the weather
They blamed it for the wars
They blamed it for the missiles
That fell like falling stars

The bird looked on regardless
It had problems of its own
With everything in such a mess
And growing chicks at home

It was on one Winter's evening
When it finally gave up the ghost
It cawed as if in mourning
And fell lifeless from its post

Heartlands

The people shouted out in glee
And desecrated the body
Hanging it up for all to see
All would now be well and jolly

But as time went by nothing changed
Everything stayed the same
And the people cast their eyes around
For something else to blame

John S. Langley

Bee Contract

As I tended my bees, I thought of Virgil
(as one does?), his Georgics, his observations
sage advice and love of 'Roman Honey'
though I'm sure the bees wouldn't have
known they were Roman

They didn't know that 'Mel' was Latin for honey
whatever the name it tasted just as sweet, their job
was to collect, store and cap enough to see the hive
through barren times

And I thought "What if the bees knew their seeking,
their feeding, their regurgitating, their tending and
their careful capping was all in vain, that all their
efforts were in the service of another

Who, choosing their moment, would open the hive
and help themselves." If they knew this would they
still carry on as they were or would they protest,
form an encampment of dissatisfied workers
outside of the hive?

Would they gather others to their cause, waggle
their wings and wave their banded abdomens like
flags or placards, refusing to fly off and forage. And,
if they did this who would they hurt most?

Heartlands

The larvae would not be fed, the nurse bees could not
nurse and the hive would begin to die. But what if the
beekeeper needed to keep the bees working?
Would he negotiate?

Would he seek to make a deal, promise to take less,
feed more, show them a little more respect? And
who would write the contract? Who from the hive
would sign it (on the Queen's behalf)?

Even if it were sealed in red propolis, would it be
legally binding? And when the time came and all the
protestors and the signatories to the agreement (the
Queen perhaps having been superseded)

Were dead and gone, who would remember the protest
or the contract or where it was kept? And would
the beekeeper forget, or pretend to forget, or would he
stick to the deal?

Perhaps he would. But if he didn't, which is more
likely, then when it came to collect the 'Frames', before
spinning out the honey, and him all dressed from head
to toe in protective clothing

I hope that some of the new bees might spy a loophole,
find a way through the small print, and make an
impression, so that this little story might still have
a sting in its tail!

John S. Langley

Peanuts

An investment in peanuts
Is all it took to produce
A bird cafe
But without the coffee
Or the croissants
Or the sandwiches

A cafe where you can choose
Whatever you want
As long as it's peanuts!

The customers flock to the table
And squabble over the pecking order
> The red-listed Green Finch
> Coal, Great, Blue and Long-tailed Tits
> Cheeky Chaffinches, argumentative Goldfinch
> Tree and hedge sparrows, the chirpy Robin
> Bright yellow Siskin and the elegant Nuthatch

But the winner is...
> The Great-Spotted Woodpecker

Resplendent in black and white
And showy splashes of red

Heartlands

It is so much bigger
It's beak, longer and stronger
It's claws, made for hanging on

But what a slovenly eater!
Throwing out bits and pieces
Willy-nilly, like a confetti of leftovers

That rain down onto the path
Where waiting scavengers
Hop around in haphazard hope

Thankful for the largesse
That falls from above
While they keep their heads down

> We watch through the window
> Safe in our double-glazed hide
> Happy to see that so little is wasted
> And wonder if any of them
> Would act any differently
> If they knew the exorbitant cost
> Of peanuts these days!

John S. Langley

Solar

A coronal mass ejection
Of plasma from the Sun

                                        Light leaves the Sun
                                        and 8minutes later

                                      Falls upon a solar panel
                                      Charges a battery

Travels 93 million miles
In 24 hours or so

            Lights the sky   Lights the room
            Auroral rainbow   Electric LED lights

                        One Sun
                        Two lights
                    One Photograph

Heartlands

John S. Langley

Snowdrops

Push up your faces to the Sun
Through the turmoil of the soil
Push through

Although your roots are sodden
Soaked through by Winter storms
Push through

Another Spring awaits your show
Of whiteness in the Borders
There'll be another Spring
Push through

Ringlet

Late June
Down in the grass
Two butterflies
Mating
Oblivious
To onlookers

Two weeks
To live
No time to lose
Resting
Just long enough
For a photograph

Before moving on
Leaving me behind
To look it up
In a reference book
And write a poem
In memoriam subito

John S. Langley

I Must Have Said The Wrong Thing

Walking nonchalantly
Feeling the sun upon my back
Next to a field full of cows
I communed with a 'Mooooo'
Deep chested and rumbly

What I wasn't expecting was:
All heads rising from the cud
All eyes, large and brown, on me
Bodies moving in my direction
An answering 'Muuuarrr'

Deeper, more guttural
Than I could ever muster
You don't realise how big cows are
Until they are coming up close
All muscle and methane

I backed away deferentially
Hoping the fence would hold
Wondering what I'd said
Determined to leave the 'Moooing'
To the experts in future...

Heartlands

John S. Langley

Same Place, Different Time
A moment in the 'Debateable Lands' between Hadrian's Wall and the current Scottish Border.

Here, before mankind
Green tropical forests flourished
Amidst a rich hum of insect wings

Here. heavy footprints were left
Hard skinned beasts in charge
Masters for millennia

Here. ice lay, many meters thick
Cleansing all that had gone before
Erasing the writing on an old page

Here, forests rose again, rivers ran
And the hand of man first lay
Upon the rough bark

Here, fires raged, tools were made
Crops were sown, children grew
And passed on their knowledge

Here, in this now quiet spot I stand
A passing shadow in dappled sunlight
Caught within a breeze

What makes You so Special?

I have thought long and hard
About what makes us special
If anything does

Dexterity/Mobility
We are the only animal
As far as we know the only animal
that has ever existed on this planet
with the ability to make fire
forge metals, mould the fundamental
elements of air, earth, fire, water
to our own ends, to make tools
to make weapons

But there are limits...
We turn our weapons upon ourselves
We deplete finite resources
We believe we can invent our way out of anything...
   ...and we're wrong!

Language
Our forms of aural communication
are formidable, passing on complex
ideas by word of mouth, coming to
a mutual understanding of a thing
Agreeing. Arguing the point.

But there are limits...
Language can lead to rage
Different languages can be barriers

John S. Langley

Writing
And recently we have learned how to record our words
so that others far away in space or time
can read what we had to say
and laugh. Or learn

But there are limits...
Recorded myth can become accepted fact
when all contemporary observers are gone.
Past meaning can be perverted for current cause.
Old knowledge can precipitate current hostility

Sociability
We can survive in large colonies,
not without friction but still..
and so we can assign communal tasks
a Baker here, a Tailor there, so that we each
do not have to do all things for ourselves
which would be very limiting

We have come to rely on others for our essentials
Food and Drink, Clothing and Shelter...
And we trade and barter and negotiate between
ourselves or intermediaries

But there are limits...
We are tribal, we develop different cultures
Different versions of perceived truth
The root of all wars

Heartlands

Creativity
We live in two worlds simultaneously.
An external world perceived through our senses.
An internal world that is all our own
to be expressed or held in secret.
From the well of our imagination springs creativity
a constant stream of ideas
on how to do things differently

But there are limits...
We do not naturally turn our minds to protect the lives
of generations yet to come.
Our creativity can lead to more efficient forms
of self-destruction

Conflict
There is perpetual conflict, based on differences
in perceived truths
>	It is my land ... No, it is mine
>	This is my right ... No, it is mine
>	God is on my side ... No, on mine

Only one thing is clear
We are born of and are bound to
the same environment
It is a silent partner
>	(and therefore easy to ignore)

This is our Eden
Will we choose to evict ourselves?

John S. Langley

Night Lights
(Brampton, Friday 10th May 2024)

Things beyond our ken
On the Sun an eruption
That would swallow our Earth
Many times over

Magnetic fields fire ions
Charged particles race
To impact our atmosphere
Molecules

Oxygen, Nitrogen get excited
Disgorging photons; Green
Pink, Blue, Purple
a new rainbow

A portent of what?
An electrical display
Science in action
Temperamental

Although we, we must wait
Until the Sun goes down
And we can see
With our human eyes

Heartlands

More or less, a wonder.
Crackling to astound
A magnificent reminder
Of impermanence...

John S. Langley

Wings

My
wings
1st moulded
from wet clay
were too fragile
for flight but served
Fluttered to entice care
Dried, cracked, fell away
Back to the succour of the soil
New wings made of wax budded
More fine detail, the rachis and barbs
Low level flight ensued but not too high
Limited by the softening, the loss of
performance as heat melted them
These wings, drip slowly away
Sink through lost childhood
Finally the feathered wings
Able to fly far and wide
To stretch and climb
Leave and return
Moving at will
Until later
Until

Heartlands

until
the feathers
begin to wear, some
unnoticed, circle and
gently fall, touching down
flight restricted, tattered
through use, wings
clipped. Contemp-
-lative of my past
flights from off
the old perch
grounded
now I
sit

John S. Langley

Spotted

After years of re-wilding
Growing long grass, hoping for flowers
On the half-managed border
We find a Spotted Orchid

Three lobed, hooded
Pale pink, with darker patches
Google confirms our ID
How did it get here?

Will it stay?
In the 'wrong' spot
Not understanding
The demarcation between

Laudable re-wilding
And a badly managed lawn…
Ah well, it knows best
And it's a beauty!

Moth?
(An unknown insect's lifecycle)

Web-tents wound in place
Eggs laid, left to find their way
Caterpillar-like

Nuisance, pest or foe
Gorging on green grown
For their purpose

Inside a chrysalis
Genes soup to form
A new body

Emergent they dry
On bare branches in bright sun
And leave on white wings

To live and return
Wind web-tents, lay fresh eggs
Turn and fly away

John S. Langley

Thistle

It's a good year for thistles
Growing like hydra, many
headed. Standing like
towers in the verges
many branched
Thorn-sharp and punk-
purple haired. Waiting for a
pollinator. Then the change to soft
thistle down and an unsteady wind to
carry hither and thither the seeds of
the next generation, looking for a
soft landing in open ground
But for now - let pink
flesh stay clear
The thistle rules the roost!

A Troubling Triptych

I.
New generations
Old habits
Nature beating Nurture
In the same house
With the same rules

II.
Looking the other way
Is like moving the deckchairs
On the Titanic

III.
Those next in line, please
Don't tinker with the paintwork
Look after the engine

John S. Langley

Ordinary?

Hawthorn blossom confetti's the path
Pink and white. Buttercups stare with
Yellow eyes from under dancing grass.

Purple and blue flowers peep out
Antennae of Cow parsley grow high
Wafting proudly their distinctive smell.

These are fleeting images from far away
That flash, disjoint, across my mind.
A waking dream, flickerings of memory

That here recall just one ordinary day.
A rainbow of greens, that words cannot
Convey. I have not the vocabulary.

Lambs cavort, run to their right mothers
At the least sign of danger, in ignorance
Of the numbers sprayed upon their fleece

Heartlands

Nettles bristle, bluebells past their best
Hug the ground and in the field the odd
black sheep knows not it's any different

There is birdsong, cows low, grass grows
As if supercharged, rain falls lightly, it is
just another day. 'There is no bad weather

Just the wrong clothing.' I smile and shiver
It is almost time for ignoring all advice
Hawthorn blossom catches in a spider's
web and sparkles like a glitter ball.

John S. Langley

How/Why?

The Chillies are starting to turn
How do they know it's time?
How do they know that they
are turning in colour
from green to red?

Can they see it?
Can they feel it?

Why do they dial up the heat
when they need their fruits to
be eaten, the seeds distributed?
Would it not put most things off!

The Chillies are starting to turn
I don't know how or why they do it!

Gathering

Swallows preparing to leave.

September the 19th
Gathered like quavers
on the telephone lines

Repeating a chorus
of chirrs and clicks
in arrowed flight

Old-timers and first-timers
consulting the memory map
of time and place

One more aerial dance
before turning South
A long way to go

Safety in numbers (I hope)
off to follow the Sun
and search for warmth

John S. Langley

Fieldfare

A flock of fieldfare clatter in the bare branches
Early arrivals in their generational relay race
From North to South, South to North, feeding
On the over-ripe redness of hawthorn berries

Chittering they climb to sit high amidst
remaining browns and yellows of obstinate
leaves, hanging on to memory, but not for long,
the ground covered with their windblown brethren

Just as the King must believe that the world smells
only of new paint, then these birds must believe
that these trees are never green, never flower, are
never full and plump and waving in a soft breeze

The Fieldfare have returned, to the same valley
the same tree, they have travelled across lesser
snowfields than their ancestors, following the
same lines of flight, young and old alike. Now

They glide down into the still-green fields, lost
amongst the sheep who cannot comprehend
the distance they have travelled and instead
bow their heads to their grazing
                              and completely ignore them…

Spider Season

It's the indoor spider season
Too cold out so they come inside
To spin their webs and sit and wait
For absent flies

And we, we clear the gossamer
Threads, with feathers bunched
And tied to straight bamboo canes
Once a week

The spiders we generally leave alone
If we see them at all, peering out from
Their crevices, or hanging upside down
From the ceiling

Captured spiders we return gingerly
To the outside, not thinking they may
Just return, under cover of darkness
To the warmth

And are we fans of these eight-legged
Hairy, many-eyed, fast moving creatures
Honed by natural selection to this peak
Of arachnid perfection?

Not a bit of it! We may admire them from
Afar, but they are not a favoured guest
Whether we share their dislike of the cold
Or not.

John S. Langley

Riddle 1

I'm third in-line and in the zone
as far as Goldilocks is concerned.
I'm a lair, but can be difficult
to reduce or rare. As a wire I'm
neither brown nor blue. Crumble
me between your fingers
What am I?

Riddle 2

I can't be seen but can be felt
though you might think me haughty.
I can hold a tune and am not afraid
to broadcast it. So let us remove
any offence, to be clear
I am everywhere
What am I?

Riddle 3

I am dangerous if left untended
though I have a place in the home.
A bullet expelled with enthusiasm, a
job lost, an impulsive nerve discharged.
Don't believe I can be tamed, I am
like passion, hanged to wait, a
neglected phase that matters
What am I?

Riddle 4

See through me, put me through my phases
I can only be broken at birth, but can run,
chatter or be still, or if you put my nose to
the grindstone I'm no slouch. Within me I
cause a reaction though when I wave it is
not in farewell. If I'm in deep I'm distressed
but a good argument holds me.
What am I?

John S. Langley

Wooden Spoon

Wooden
A handmade spoon
Carved from sycamore
Shaped roughly at first
Then smoothed and oiled
To bring out the grain
Natural beauty to be
retained. Thrice
over sanded
finely to
form a
utensil
New life
from old
to hold in
hand, to
buy and
to take
home
use

Seeing is Believing

I remember it was a Tuesday
A rainy day with a strong breeze

The street was silvered slick
Puddled with oily rainbows

So I didn't see it at first
Hiding away in an alley

Forlorn and bedraggled
Eyes shining in streetlights

In fear and self-knowledge
I'm sure it didn't notice me

Though it froze for a moment
Before going on its way

I'm sure I know what I saw
But you'd never believe me!

John S. Langley

The Pen and The Word

John S. Langley

Mastering Words!

A master of words can misbehave
and decide to boldly go beyond
the split infinitive when fancy
drives the imagination!

Knowing the correct use of grammar
means that punctuation; that strange
art, of infinite variety, can be played
like a fish that always slips the net!

But woe betide the amateur who
with wanton disregard to form
gushes forth their inner thoughts
upon a virgin page!

Let those who quibble heed only this -

That each slip from the golden rules
is boldly made and thoughtfully
intended and, like Van Gogh's
Sunflowers, is there for art's sake!

And even more, if more be needed
remember that these 'golden rules'
are less than three full centuries old
so remind them of that - and leave them cold!

Show No Fear

Show no fear, the teacher said
Be confident, act it if you must
Don't tremble, sweat or show weakness
They can sense it like a pack of wolves
That scent an injured prey

Thanks, I said, wondering what
I'd let myself in for, bringing poetry
Into schools had seemed so noble a venture
In theory, but now? The door ahead
Cracked open, sunlight shone through

And the Assembly Hall echoed
With the multitudinous voices
Of gathering minds into which cauldron
I was about to descend, **alone!**
My palms were damp

There was no way back
The door closed behind me
Silence was called for, all eyes on me
I swallowed hard, 'show no fear'
I thought, though I knew that
A pack of 4 and 5 year olds
Can smell fear!

John S. Langley

Don't Wait!

I know this ditty isn't up to the normal standard required for an anthology like this! My excuse is that it was written for a Primary school Rotary Poetry Prizegiving that I was asked to participate in. I wanted to read something that would inspire the young audience to write poetry; a kind of 'Anyone can do it if they try', a 'Have a go' and a 'I'm sure you could do better than this!'. What I was not expecting was the spontaneous, loud, burst of applause that I got at the end! ... Ah, kids, don't you just luv 'em...

I almost wrote a poem today
But then I just forgot
It was going to be really good
And have a super plot

I nearly wrote a poem today
I had it in my head
But I didn't write it down, you see
I watched TV instead

I think I'll write a poem tomorrow
I'm pretty sure I will
I'll wait until I feel inspired
Then pages I will fill

With dragons and cars and big brown cows
My mind will be racing then
Oh, hold on... I've got an idea right now
I'll go and get my pen...

Seeking Inspiration

Here I sit, seeking that particular word
Around which my poem will pivot

My nibbed pen is charged with Indian ink
And awaits instruction

Shall it be 'Love' or 'Peace' or 'Hope'
Or shall I write of darker things

No less real

A drop of black falls from my tired nib
And settles onto the snowfield

Of blank paper, forming a perfect circle
and a risen dome

Convex, complex, it glints in the light
and, like a crow's eye,
stares back at me...

John S. Langley

Finding The Right Word

Ma rhythm's a problem, ma rhyming is too
I'm writing a song but feeling kinda blue
There just ain't the words for me an' ma news
Cos I want to sing it meaningful, I want to sing the Blues

I can't find the right thing, but I'm looking for clues
To rhyme with ma feelings, what have I got to loose?
Should I choose to schmoose like my best pair of shoes?
Or cruise in the mews on the way to Syracuse?

Do I take ma cues from the ma lazy, crazy muse
or just settle down for an hour's quiet snooze?
I must find the right thing to rhyme with my blues
So as not to accuse, or enthuse, as that might confuse

Or abuse or bemuse, I'd rather amuse
As I've got no tattoos, I might get reviews
But you'll have to excuse me, I'll have to refuse
I just can't find the right word, to rhyme with ma Blues

I can't find the right word
I can't find the right word
To rhyme with ma Blues...

Legerdemain

Light of hands
Engaged in subterfuge
Given over to the
English from the French in
Rapidly performed illusions
Delivered as if by magic
Entertaining and clever
Made to look impossible
And provide distractions
In a world of wonder
Needing a denouement

*A hiding of the truth, a sleight of hand,
as part of a performance perhaps.*

John S. Langley

Life's Work

Having slaved away
moulding a poem
from life's experiential
clay

Choosing each word
it's placement, rhythm
meaning, so as to strike
a chord

I fashioned art from
out of the ether, tended
it, grew it into shape
and form

Until, half-satisfied,
which is the best that
I can reasonably hope
I laid

it aside, as being as
complete as I could
make it

After further months of toil
there in my hand
lay an artifact

Heartlands

Oh joy! Oh wonder
of delight! Oh relief
that such a thing had
taken flight!

Later a number of copies
lay upon a craft stall
Table

In amongst more worthy
tomes, priced upon a
Label

A lady took one in her hand
not knowing it was I who
wrote it

Perused, flicked through
glanced fleetingly
within

'I'm looking for a present,'
she said, 'I don't like poetry
very much

but I think I'll go for this one.'
As she paid she looked me
in the eye

'After all,' she said, 'it
might not be any good
but at least it's cheap!'

John S. Langley

Bon Voyage

I've got nothing to say
I've got writer's block
But a friend of mine said
(and it came as a shock)
"Just pick up your pen
or go to your screen
do it quite often
and make it routine.
Scribble down whatever
comes into your mind
you can go back to it later
but always be kind."

I think of these words
as I sit here and write
I feel the block shifting
perhaps she was right
So this nonsense I give
as a message to all
just like you get up
when you've had a big fall
Don't give in, don't give up
just answer the call
Keep on with your writing
Bon voyage to you all!

Halfway Mark

Halfway to a new collection
Poems written, shy of recollection
Gathered into a personal file
Varying in their tone and style

Halfway is a good place to be
It's all downhill from here, you see
Although there's editing to do
Looking again from a different view

A significant point has been reached
Time to consider what it should be called
Before finally letting it be unleashed
On an unsuspecting world…

John S. Langley

Spilt!

The book
in its protective wrapper
is now at a safe distance
and I can lift
the mischievous cup
once again
from its deceptively
friendly coaster
carefully, this time
without fear
of the liquid
slipping uncontrolled
and unbidden
over the lip

I sip
cautiously
the book lies
flat and safe
more than a splash
or an accidental spill
away, from where it
glances at me
from the corner
of its literary eye
disapprovingly

Heartlands

Coffee
stains
hot coffee scalds
nothing destroys a book
more effectively
than water
however flavoured

I do not return its look
but sip from the bitter cup
of penance
try to reinvigorate
my shaken intent
to rebuild broken bridges
smooth ruffled pages
so that we are able
to look each other
in the eye
once more
and, in time
I can allow myself
another coffee

John S. Langley

Afterlife

They didn't sell until after you died
Benjamin
Boxed and put away
A little rough around the edges
Signed

It was after you were gone
They were excavated, brought out
Cobwebs cleared away
To find that the words were still there
Signed

Then they sold in an instant
A flurry of online payments
What couldn't be sold before
Was consumed afterwards
In gulps

I hope that they are read
I hope you will be remembered
For the words that you wrote
And signed

Note: *An Independent Bookseller had a box of signed books by Benjamin Zephaniah that were unfortunately a little tattered, each affected to a greater or lesser extent. The whole was deemed unsaleable and put away 'in storage'. After Benjamin passed away the bookseller retrieved these damaged books, offering them for sale but expecting them not to sell. They sold out in minutes!*

Heartbeat

Written in tune with the heart
Rhythm and rhyme play their part
Echoing down through the line
Each beat comes one at a time

And so it goes on through the years
Resonance of our shared cares
Words written by one in their time
When read by others still chime

Through differences down to the core
A reminder of what it is for
That we think and we breathe and are gone
But at heart we are beating as one

John S. Langley

Fiction From Fact

An author can speak
Through their character's mouths
Taking different sides
In the same argument

Keeping a distance
From an opinion expressed
Against the grain
Dodging a social bullet

Or say farewell through fiction
More real than the world
More heartfelt than emotion
Before it's too late

Note: *Terry Pratchett took such an opportunity in his last Discworld novel 'The Shepherd's Crown' – after he was diagnosed with a form of dementia.*

Connecting

I write these words
In ignorance
Of your presence

The eyes that scan
These words
The mind

That translates
Them into
Meaning

For a moment
Resurrects
Me

This is the power
Of the written word

John S. Langley

Haiku

I write poetry
To capture a memory
Before it is lost

www.ingramcontent.com/pod-product-compliance
Lightning Source LLC
Chambersburg PA
CBHW061735070526
44585CB00024B/2682